WORLD IN VIEW
ISRAEL
Mike Rogoff

STECK-VAUGHN
L I B R A R Y
Austin, Texas

Library of Congress Cataloging-in-Publication Data

Rogoff, Mike, 1946–
   Israel / Mike Rogoff.
     p.   cm.—(World in view)
   "First published 1990 by Macmillan Children's Books"—T.p. verso.
   Includes index.
   Summary: Surveys the history, climate, geography, political
situation, people, languages, agriculture, economics, education, and
lifestyles of Israel.
   ISBN 0-8114-2432-4
   1. Israel—Juvenile literature. [1. Israel.] I. Title.
II. Series.
DS102.95.R64   1991
956.94—dc20   90-10027
                                             CIP
                                           AC

Cover: *View of Jerusalem showing the Dome of the Rock, a Muslim
temple in the center, Christian churches in the background, and the
Jewish Mount Olive cemetery in the foreground.*

Title page: *The Dead Sea is so salty that people float without any effort.*

Designed by Julian Holland Publishing Ltd
Picture research by Mike Rogoff

Typeset by Multifacit Graphics, Keyport, NJ
Printed and bound in the United States
by Lake Book, Melrose Park, IL
1 2 3 4 5 6 7 8 9 0 LB 95 94 93 92 91

Photographic credits Cover: Leo de Wys, Inc. © Steve Vidler, title page: Jewish National
Fund, 7 C.J. Lederman, 8, 9, 12 Jewish National Fund, 21 Shai Ginott, 23 Jewish National
Fund, 24 Miri Adini, 25 Jewish National Fund, 28 Israel Government Press Office, 29 Jewish
National Fund, 31 Israel Government Press Office, 32 Jewish National Fund, 33 Israel
Government Press Office, 36, 39 Jewish National Fund, 40, 45, 49, 52, 56, 57, 61, 64, 65, 67,
69, 73, 75, 76 Israel Government Press Office, 77 Israel Aircraft Industries, 78 M. Rogoff, 80,
81, 82 Jewish National Fund, 84, 87 Israel Government Press Office, 88 Shai Ginott, 89, 91, 92
Israel Government Press Office

Contents

ISRAEL

LEBANON
Mt. Hermon
9,145 ft.

Golan Heights (HaGolan)

Bay of Haifa
Haifa ●

L. Hula

SYRIA

Galilee ●
L. Tiberias
(Sea of Galilee)

Mt. Carmel ▲
528m
Tiberias ●
● Nazareth

Qishon R.

Plains of Sharon

National Water Course

Mediterranean

Sea

● Beyt Shean

Samaria

Faria R.

0 miles   50

0 km   50

TEL AVIV
(Jaffa)
Bat Yam ●
Holon ●

Yarqon R.

Peta Tiqwa
Ramat
Gan

Nablus ●

Sarida R.

Jordan R.

Lakhish R.

Soreq R.

Negev Conduit

Shefela

Jericho ●

Jerusalem ●

Bethlehem ●

● Hebron ● Judaea

Dead Sea
(Yam Hamelah)

Gaza ● Strip

Gaza

Ha besor

Gerar

H a d a r o m

Beer ● Beersheba
Sheva

Hamakhtesh
Hamakhtesh Haqatan
Hagadol

JORDAN

N e g e v

es Siq

EGYPT

Makhtesh
Ramon

D e s e r t

Sinai
Desert

Biq'at 'Uvda

● Eilat

4

1   Introducing Israel

Israel is known to many as the Holy Land. It is the land described in the Bible, where the tribes of Israel settled over 3,200 years ago. It was the homeland of Jesus of Nazareth, and the place where Christianity was born. It is also the place from which Mohammed, the founder of Islam, rose to heaven.

Since 1948 Israel has been an independent state. It is a small country, slightly larger than the state of Massachusetts. It is at the eastern end of the Mediterranean Sea and forms part of the region of Asia, commonly referred to as the Middle East. Governed from the ancient city of Jerusalem, Israel's population in 1988 totaled about 4.4 million.

The map of Israel

The Mediterranean coastline forms the entire western side of Israel. To the north lies the Republic of Lebanon, and to the northeast lies the Arab Republic of Syria. In the east, Israel shares a very long border with the Hashemite Kingdom of

The national flag of Israel is white with two blue stripes running across it, and a six-pointed star, the Shield of David, in the center. The national anthem is called *Hatikvah*, which means "The Hope." Composed in 1878, it was adopted as the national anthem at the eighteenth Zionist Congress in 1933, 15 years before Israel itself was born.

5

DISTRICTS OF ISRAEL

LEBANON

SYRIA

Mediterranean

Sea

Occupied Territories

Sea of Galilee

Haifa

NORTHERN

Nazareth

Golan Heights (Ha Golan)

Plain of Sharon

HAIFA

0 miles   50

0 km   50

Tel Aviv
TEL AVIV

CENTRAL

Ramla

Occupied

West Bank

Territories

JERUSALEM

Jerusalem

Gaza Strip

Dead Sea

Beersheba

I S R A E L

JORDAN

SOUTHERN

E G Y P T

Negev Desert

Sinai Desert

Jordan. Almost half that border runs along the Jordan River and through the Dead Sea. To the south and southwest another long border separates Israel from the Sinai Desert, which belongs to the Arab Republic of Egypt.

Israel is long but quite narrow. It is about 280 miles from the northern village of Metulla, on the Lebanese border, to the southern city of Eilat, on the Red Sea. At its widest, near the desert city of Beersheba, the country is only 110 miles from east to west. Israel's area is 8,017 square miles.

In addition to Israel's own territory, there are the Occupied Territories which have been under Israeli control since the Six-Day War of 1967. These include the Golan Heights in the northeast, the Gaza Strip along the Mediterranean coast in the southwest, and the large, mountainous West

The ancient Mediterranean port of Acre was once one of the greatest in the region. Today the harbor is used by fishing boats and pleasure craft only. The lone tower at the bottom of the picture, and part of the city's sea walls, are 800 years old.

The spring of Ein Kelt in the barren Judean Desert creates a magnificent oasis and offers a welcome rest stop for hikers. The canyon was once a route for travelers between Jerusalem and Jericho.

Bank region, to the north and south of Jerusalem. Between this West Bank of the Jordan River and the Mediterranean Sea at Netanya, Israel has a narrow waist of only 9 miles.

Between two continents

Israel belongs to the continent of Asia, but neighboring Egypt forms part of Africa. Israel is located on the thin piece of land where the two continents meet, and forms a bridge between them.

For thousands of years, travelers between Africa and Asia had to cross Israel. Most roads followed the valleys and the easier mountain passes. They avoided rough ground and difficult hazards such as sand dunes and swamps. Fresh drinking water was essential to the traveler. Israel lacks plentiful water supplies. Every spring, stream, and well was jealously guarded as a source of life. People sometimes fought over these water supplies. The Bible describes just such an incident in ancient times:

And Isaac's servants digged in the valley, and found there a well of springing water. And the herdmen of Gerar did strive with Isaac's herdmen, saying, "The water is ours..." (Genesis 26:19)

Ancient cities were often built along the highways, near springs or other sources of water, in positions that could easily be defended.

Salt formations at the Dead Sea, the lowest point on Earth. A glass of this water is one-third salt! Bathers in the Dead Sea simply cannot sink.

9

The shape of the land

Jerusalem, the nation's seat of government, sits 2,600 feet high in the Judean Mountain Range, and only about 38 miles inland from the Mediterranean coast. Mountains form the country's backbone. They stretch north, as the Samarian Range, to the edge of Galilee, and extend southward to the Negev Desert.

To the east of the mountains lies the Judean Desert, an extremely dry, hot, and rocky region. In a half-hour drive through the desert you can descend to the shore of the Dead Sea, the saltiest body of water in the world. The Dead Sea is special in another way. It lies 1,300 feet below the level of the ocean, and is therefore the lowest point on the surface of the Earth.

Traveling west from the mountains, the roads descend more gradually through hill country until they reach the flat Coastal Plain. The plain is as wide as 15 miles to the south of Tel Aviv, but as narrow as several hundred feet farther north at Haifa.

The Lower Galilee region, in the north of the country, is made up of chains of hills with farming valleys between them. In the east these hills drop steeply to the Sea of Galilee, which is known in the Hebrew language as Lake Kinneret. Although called a "sea," this body of water is actually a freshwater lake. The Jordan River flows into it from the north, and leaves it again in the south.

In the far north of the country is the Upper Galilee region, with its canyons and wild mountain scenery. The eastern part of this region takes in the low-lying, extremely fertile Hula Valley, where the Jordan River rises. The Golan

Heights overlook the Hula Valley from the east. Just north of the Golan Heights is Mount Hermon, the highest mountain in the entire area. Its highest peak, 9,145 feet above sea level, is in neighboring Syria, but other important peaks stretch southward in Israeli territory.

The Negev Desert takes up most of the southern half of the country. On a map it looks like a huge upside-down triangle. The northern part of the Negev is covered with powdery, yellow soil, which is in fact very fertile. This wind-blown earth is called loess. Farther south are bare mountains, canyons, and three huge craters known as cirques. The bottom tip of the triangle touches the Gulf of Aqaba, the eastern arm of the Red Sea.

A crack in the Earth

A unique feature of Israel is a long, deep split in the surface of the Earth. Geographers call it the Great Syrian-African Rift Valley. It runs along the entire eastern edge of the country from north to south, in an almost straight line. The Rift is marked by the Hula Valley, the Sea of Galilee, the Jordan Valley, the Dead Sea, a long strip of desert called the Arava, and the extremely deep waters of the Gulf of Aqaba.

The Rift Valley was formed long ago, when huge plates of rock that were sections of the Earth's crust moved away from each other. This caused massive upheavals and earthquakes that pushed up the rocks to form many of the mountains seen today. This cracking of the Earth's crust allowed hot, mineral-rich water to reach the surface as springs, especially in the

11

regions of the Sea of Galilee and the Dead Sea. The health-giving powers of these springs were discovered more than 2,000 years ago. Today, relaxing hot baths have been built at these spots.

Beneath the ground
Almost all of Israel is covered by the kind of rocks known as limestone. Geologists believe that in the distant past Israel was flooded by the ocean many times. Each flood lasted millions of years, with millions of years in between. In each flood, minerals and dead shellfish sank to the ocean floor, where they formed layers of sediment. In the dry periods these hardened into layers of sedimentary rocks.

The hardness of different limestone rocks depends on how old they are and on what

The Sorek Cave, in the mountains west of Jerusalem, was formed by water eroding the limestone rocks. Later, dripping water in the cave deposited other limestone in fantastic stalactite and stalagmite formations.

The famous Solomon's Pillars at Timna, north of Eilat, are huge, natural red-sandstone formations. Very close by, a small 3,400-year-old Egyptian temple was found, for the worship of Hathor, the goddess of the copper miners. The copper mines of Timna are older than those of Solomon, mentioned in the Bible.

minerals they contain. Some, such as chalk, are soft. They were carved out by ancient people as shelters and burial caves. Other limestone rocks, such as dolomite, are hard. These were quarried for building stones.

The Golan Heights once had active volcanoes which spread molten lava over the limestone

13

rocks. The lava hardened into a black-brown rock called basalt, and this covers a broad area in the northeast of the country.

At the country's southern tip, near Eilat, are jagged granite mountains. These are the oldest rocks in the area. They form the edge of a huge block of such mountains found in nearby Sinai and Saudi Arabia. In the same area are cliffs of deep-red sandstone. Winds and winter floods have carved out fantastic formations and narrow canyons in the sandstone. Copper has been mined from these rocks since ancient times.

Mild winters, dry summers

Israel's climate is of the type known as Mediterranean. The winters are mild and rainy, and the summers are hot and dry. In fact, the country receives no rain at all between May and September. Seventy percent of the rain falls between November and February. Jerusalem, for example, has virtually the same climate as San Francisco, California, with about 20 inches of rain falling over 50-60 days during the winter rainy season. ·

It is a general rule that more rain falls in the north of Israel than in the south, and more in the west than in the east. The rainiest areas, therefore, are the Coastal Plain and the Galilee Mountains in the northwest, and the driest are the deserts of the south and east. Although these desert areas get very little rain, a cloudburst even in distant hills can send powerful flash floods rushing down desert valleys and canyons.

In the winter, snow can be expected in the high mountain areas, but it is often light, and does not fall every year. Elsewhere, it is almost unheard of. The Coastal Plain has had no snow since a freak winter in 1950.

The hot summers are quite tolerable in high mountain areas like Jerusalem, which is quite dry. However, they are stickier and less comfortable on the humid Coastal Plain. On a typical summer's day in Jerusalem or Tel Aviv, the temperature will be between about 82°F and 95°F. It will be about 9°F hotter on the Dead Sea or in Eilat.

Because of Israel's mild climate, the change from autumn to winter, and from winter to spring, is not as clearly marked as in places like North America or northern Europe, where the winters may be snowy and very cold. Spring and autumn are normally very pleasant seasons with many pleasant days everywhere in the country. There are occasional days in late spring and autumn, however, when hot, dry, dusty air moves in from the eastern desert and sends the temperatures shooting up. This wind is known as the *sharay* in Hebrew, and as the *hamsin* in Arabic.

2 Out and About

Despite Israel's small size, it has a surprising variety of landscape. In many areas it is only a short drive from wooded mountain slopes to bare deserts, or rich farmland to rocky canyons. Each region has its own special scenery, plant life, and wild animals. The regional differences are often determined by climate, by the landscape and its geology, and by the amount of water available.

Looking after nature
In Israel, any land area that is particularly beautiful, or that is the home of unusual kinds of plants or animals, may be declared an official nature reserve. A national organization called the Nature Reserves Authority is then responsible for the protection and upkeep of the reserve. This might involve preparing hiking trails, information centers, and facilities for visitors. Many natural areas are still waiting for official approval as nature reserves. When that happens, the total number of reserves will be 414. They will cover almost 25 percent of Israel's total land area.

Water for life
Israel's poor water supply can cause problems. There are very few rivers or large springs, and the southern deserts can get as little as two to four inches of rain a year. Nevertheless, Israel is the most efficient country in the world in terms of how much of its available water resources it manages to use. Much of the water reaches the thirsty towns through the huge pipes of the

Rosh Hanikra is a series of beautiful grottoes carved out of white chalk cliffs by the crashing waves of the Mediterranean Sea. The grottoes are located near Israel's northern border. They are placed in a protected area and are reached by cable car.

National Water Carrier. This system pumps water from the low-lying Sea of Galilee to a geographical high point from which the water can begin flowing south.

Along the way, the system brings in the water of many other springs and reservoirs. At the same time it distributes water to towns, industry, and

17

The waterfall of the Banias stream is one of the sources of the Jordan River in Upper Galilee. Ancient ruins have been found nearby of a Hellenistic shrine of the god Pan, and of the town of Caesarea Philippi mentioned in the New Testament.

farms as far south as the Negev Desert. The Jordan River, which runs into the Sea of Galilee, is also tapped farther upstream for local needs. No one owns the water on private land. In a country where water is so precious, all sources belong to the nation. Farmers may use their own supply, but only as part of an agreed amount they are allowed each year.

There are other ways of increasing the water supply. Israel has developed new techniques for desalination. This process takes the salt out of sea water so that it can be drunk. This is an expensive process, however, and is usually used only when there is no other water available, as in Eilat. Another method is to use an airplane to "seed" rain clouds with certain chemical crystals. This can increase rainfall in some areas by as much as 25 percent. Often city sewage water can be purified enough to be used for irrigating, or watering, certain crops.

Bringing back the forests
Once upon a time Israel was covered by large forests of oak, pine, and terebinth. As recently as 100 years ago there were still many wooded areas. These have almost all gone now.

For thousands of years armies, marching between Egypt and the rich river valleys of the Tigris and Euphrates in Mesopotamia, would cut down trees for their campfires and siege-machines. Woods would be cleared so that the enemy was denied any natural cover. Farmers also cleared away trees to increase their farmland. Nomads burned down woods to provide grazing areas for their flocks. During World War I Turkish soldiers cut down much of the forest that remained to build their railroad lines and fuel their locomotives.

At the beginning of this century, Israel was called Palestine. Jewish settlers started to arrive in Palestine about a hundred years ago and began to reclaim land. They and later settlers turned wilderness into farmland by draining swamps, removing boulders, and terracing hillsides. They also replanted many forests that had been destroyed. Many were financed by the Jewish National Fund (JNF). In the last 80 years the JNF has planted about 185 million trees throughout the country, half of them in the last 20 years. Three million new trees are planted every year. Most of the new trees are pine and cypress, but oak, eucalyptus, carob, and other trees have been planted too.

Five percent of Israel is now covered in forest once again. The trees' roots help to secure the topsoil and prevent it from being blown away. The new forests provide shelter for many small animals as well as attractive recreation areas for people.

Trees and plants
Israel has an amazing variety of trees, plants, and flowers. This is due to the different zones of climate within the country. About 2,250 plant species have been identified. By comparison, England, which is six times the size of Israel, has only 1,700 species.

Israel's Mediterranean zone includes most of the hill country and the Coastal Plain. These are the most densely populated areas. The rainfall encourages forests and dense bush, although the original forests have only survived in a couple of mountain areas. Inland, low rainfall zones such as the Lower Jordan Valley and the edges of the Judean Desert, have only scrub and low bushes.

Desert zones make up the southern and eastern parts of Israel. Here, plants and trees fight for their survival. Deep roots seek water far underground. Small leaves cut down water loss from many desert plants. Thorns, bitter sap, or tough bark protect trees from hungry animals.

Within these desert areas are a few spots where fresh springs combine with the great heat to produce subtropical conditions. Jericho and Ein Gedi, near the Dead Sea, are the best examples of these oases. The lotus tree, the giant reed, and the

The rare wild black iris of Mount Gilboa, overlooking the Jezre'el Valley, attracts many nature-lovers in the spring. The Society for the Protection of Nature has been very successful in teaching the public to enjoy wild flowers, but not to pick them.

unusual Sodom apple grow here. In ancient times the people who lived in these oases cultivated the balsam tree, which was used to make perfume and a fragrant ointment called balm.

Everywhere in the country, in any season, wild flowers can be found. In early spring, however, when a spell of warm weather may follow the rains, the whole countryside bursts into color. Especially beautiful are the hillsides of Galilee, with their fields of blood-red poppies and anemones, and all kinds of white, yellow, and purple wild flowers.

Watching birds and animals
In ancient times there were many more kinds of large wild animals in Israel than there are today.

The Bible, for example, mentions lions, tigers, bears, wild oxen, ostriches, and several kinds of deer. They have all been hunted down and none survives.

Leopards were also thought to be extinct. A few years ago, however, hikers in the Ein Gedi area of the Judean Desert came home with exciting stories. They said they had seen leopards, and had photographs to prove it. Scientists and nature-lovers have been keeping track of these magnificent big cats ever since, in order to learn more about them.

Foxes, wolves, jackals, hyenas, and several species of small wild cat still exist, but they are few in number, and anyway are mostly active at night. Antelope roam the Golan Heights, and parts of Lower Galilee and the Negev Desert. Their numbers have grown so much that they have become a real nuisance to farmers. The ibex, a kind of wild goat, is seen on rocks and cliffs in the desert. The wild boar is still found in some wooded areas of the north, and the water buffalo survives in the swamps of the Hula Nature Reserve.

An unusual game reserve called Hai-Bar has been created in the Arava Desert, north of Eilat. Its aim is to bring back some of the animals that have disappeared from the country, and allow them to thrive in a spacious natural environment. These include ostriches and wild asses, and rare antelopes such as the addax and the oryx. Most of the animals were brought from Africa, where such species are still found in the wild. Some that have adapted well have been freed in the Negev to roam as their ancestors did.

Ibex or wild goats on the edge of the gigantic Ramon Crater in the Negev Desert. A protected species, they have almost lost their fear of people.

Israel is an exciting place for birdwatchers. Water birds are found along the coast and near fish-breeding ponds. Eagles, vultures, and hawks make their homes in high cliffs. Other species prefer farmland or towns. In addition, Israel is visited twice a year by millions of birds migrating from Europe and Asia to the warm continent of Africa. They fly south in the winter and return north in the spring. They include storks, pelicans, and birds of prey. On the way, many stop to rest in Israel. Altogether about 350 bird species can be spotted in the country.

Reptiles such as lizards are cold-blooded, and so they enjoy Israel's long months of warm sunshine. There are about 80 reptile species. Snakes are not very common, and only the cobra

23

The magical world of the coral reefs is seen in the Red Sea near Eilat. The amazing colors and the variety of fish, corals, and plant life make this one of nature's real wonders.

and two kinds of viper are venomous. There used to be crocodiles in a small river between Tel Aviv and Haifa until about 80 years ago. They have since disappeared, but today a few crocodile and alligator farms still exhibit these huge beasts.

Although Israel has many types of freshwater and sea fish that make excellent eating, fishing is not a major industry. The coastal waters of Israel are very deep, and large-scale fishing is not easy. Popular fish of the Mediterranean include types of grouper, bream, mullet, snapper, and sole. The freshwater Sea of Galilee gives carp, sardines, and the famous St. Peter's fish, while trout swim in the upper reaches of the Jordan River. Most fascinating for snorkelers and scuba-divers are the spectacular tropical fish of the Red Sea coral reefs, which are said to be among the most varied and colorful in the world.

3 An Ancient Land

In prehistoric times, people lived by hunting wild animals and gathering wild plants. They roamed about in their search for food, and took shelter in caves. Scientists have found many bones and stone tools in Israel that suggest humans were living there over a million years ago.

People later learned how to grow crops and to tame animals. Farming settlements first grew up in the fertile river valleys of the Middle East, along the Nile, the Tigris, and the Euphrates. Many important developments occurred in Israel itself. Jericho must have been one of the first cities in the world, as parts of it date back 10,000 years. By 3200 B.C. other great cities such as Ur, in what is now Iraq, had grown up. Israel was in an important position between these new civilizations.

The subtropical oasis town of Jericho. The low hill in the center of the picture is the tell, where remains of the world's oldest city were discovered. The city was captured by Joshua and the tribes of Israel around 1250 B.C.

25

In cities such as Jericho, people learned to make pottery and to work metal. Weapons were made from copper. This was later mixed with other metals to make bronze. New methods of farming and irrigating crops allowed farmers to sell their produce. Traders traveled through Israel as they passed between the empires of the Middle East, such as Assyria, Babylon, and Egypt. In times of war, however, large armies traveled along the same routes, bringing destruction and suffering.

The land of the Bible
Our knowledge of the region's history comes from several sources. Archaeologists have dug up ancient buildings and other remains. About 5,000 years ago people learned to write. They could describe events and record laws. Historians can study these records to find out about past civilizations.

The most useful source for historians is the Bible. This is a collection of ancient books describing the history and the way of life of the Jews in ancient times. It is a holy book to Jews, who call its first five books the Torah. It forms the Old Testament of the Christian Bible. Many of the religious preachers and wonder workers described in the Bible as "prophets" are revered by Muslims as well as by Christians and Jews.

The Bible describes the forefathers of the Jewish people as "patriarchs." The first was Abraham, who was said to have been born in Ur. There was his son Isaac, and his grandson Jacob, who was later given the name Israel. They may have lived over 3,500 years ago in Canaan, as the land of Israel was then known. They worshiped a single God, at a time when most people worshiped many different gods.

Famine drove the descendants of the patriarchs, known as Israelites, to Egypt. They settled there, but in about 1500 B.C. they were enslaved by the rulers of Egypt. A leader called Moses led them from Egypt, and they wandered in the desert for 40 years. Jews and Christians believe that on Mount Sinai, Moses received a set of laws known as the Ten Commandments from God.

Conquest and defeat

The Israelites believed that the land of Canaan had been promised to them by God. Under a leader named Joshua, they invaded parts of Canaan in about 1250 B.C. They met fierce resistance from the people living there, but their chief enemies were the Philistines, who lived on the fertile plains of the Mediterranean coast.

There were 12 tribes of Israelites. For 200 years they were governed and led into war by local

Digging Up the Past
How do archaeologists begin their search for past civilizations? In the Middle East, very ancient cities can be identified by a flat-topped hill, shaped like a loaf of bread. This mound is called a tell. A tell is an artificial hill that grew higher and higher over the ages as people built a new city on the ruins of the one before. As archaelogists dig down through the tell they uncover layer after layer of remains, each older than the one before. They search for vital clues. Even fragments of pottery are useful, for they help to identify the date of each layer.

Visiting American school-children wade through the water of the Siloam or Hezekiah's Tunnel. Built during the Assyrian invasion of 701 B.C. to bring springwater into the city, the tunnel winds 582 yards through solid rock.

leaders such as Deborah, Gideon, and Samson. These leaders were known as "judges." The tribes eventually united under a king called Saul to fight the Philistines. The next king was named David. He was a strong and popular leader. He defeated the Philistines and also captured the city of Jerusalem, which he made his capital. David's son, Solomon, was famous for his wisdom. He developed trade and built the great temple in Jerusalem. However, when Solomon died, the kingdom split in two. The ten northern tribes formed a new Kingdom of Israel, while the two southern tribes, still based in Jerusalem, formed the Kingdom of Judah.

In 721 B.C., the northern Kingdom of Israel was destroyed by Assyria, one of the great empires of the Middle East. The survivors were taken prisoner, and all trace of them was lost. Judah held out. However, the Assyrians were defeated in their turn by armies from Babylon, a kingdom lying between the Tigris and Euphrates rivers. In 586 B.C., Babylon defeated the Kingdom of Judah, and a large part of the population was taken eastward into exile.

The great Old Testament city of Bet She' an in the Upper Jordan Valley lies under the grassy hill at the top of the picture. The well-preserved semicircular theater at the bottom, and the newly discovered wide streets in the center, are from the Roman and Byzantine periods when the city was known as Scythopolis.

Persians, Greeks, and Jews

Babylon was finally defeated by the mighty empire of the Persians in 539 B.C. The Jews were allowed to return from exile. They rebuilt the city of Jerusalem, including its great temple.

In 334 B.C. Alexander the Great crossed into Asia from Europe. This young general was from Macedonia, in northern Greece. In just a few years he conquered the Persian empire and led his armies into India. Alexander died in 323 B.C., but his armies now controlled most of the Middle East and Egypt.

The Greek way of life, known as Hellenism, took root in the region. Many Jews were attracted by Hellenism, with its theater, athletics, and philosophy. Other Jews felt that Hellenism posed a threat to Jewish religious beliefs and morality. A long, bitter struggle broke out between the two factions. In 167 B.C. many Jews rose in revolt against the ruler, Antiochus IV, who had outlawed the Jewish religion altogether. The Jews were led by a family called the Maccabees. They won their independence, and to this day Jews celebrate the victory with the festival of Chanukah. For a century the old Jewish kingdom, now renamed Judea, was brought back into existence.

Herod and Jesus

In 63 B.C., the Romans marched into Judea, and added it to their huge empire. In 47 B.C., the Romans appointed an Idumean who followed the Jewish religion as governor of the Galilee region. He was a ruthless young man called Herod. As a result of civil war in the country, Herod was

King Herod's great mountain-top palace of Masada. Its incredible strength as a fortress kept the Romans out until A.D. 73. The three "steps" of Herod's Northern Palace can be seen on the left side of the picture.

forced to flee to Rome. The Roman ruler Mark Antony was impressed by Herod, and gave him the title of King of the Jews. The Jews were less impressed, however, and resisted Herod. It took him two years to fight his way back to Jerusalem. Herod ruled Judea for 33 years. He built great cities, fortresses, ports, and water systems. In Jerusalem he rebuilt the temple. It was now so grand that it became one of the architectural wonders of the world.

When Herod died in 4 B.C., the country was divided up among his sons. Jerusalem and the central region came under the direct rule of a Roman governor, or procurator. Jews believed that God would send a special person called the

31

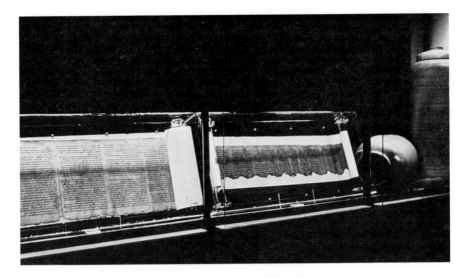

The Dead Sea Scrolls, found in a desert cave by a nomad shepherd boy in 1947, are the most important "find" ever made in Israel. Written over 2,000 years ago by a small Jewish sect called Essenes, some scrolls contain parts of the Old Testament, while others are special "books" of the Essene community. The extreme dryness of the Dead Sea region allowed the parchment to survive.

Messiah who would expel the Romans and bring them new hope.

Groups formed, each with its own ideas about the future of Judea. One such group was the Essenes. We know a lot about the Essenes as fragments of scrolls of their writings were discovered in a cave near the Dead Sea in 1947.

Another group followed Jesus of Nazareth. Jesus had grown up in the Galilee region, and here he taught and healed the sick. He also came to Jerusalem, and soon had many followers. Some thought he was the Messiah and the Son of God. Others thought he was a great teacher, or rabbi. The Romans, however, saw Jesus as a troublemaker. They understood that a Messiah would claim to be King of the Jews, and under Roman law that was treason. The penalty was death by crucifixion. Scholars believe that the year of Jesus's death was A.D. 29.

This fishing boat from the time of Jesus was retrieved intact from the mud of the Sea of Galilee. It is unique. Over 27 feet long, it was discovered when a number of drought years caused the level of the lake to drop.

War with Rome

The Jews suffered great hardship under Roman rule. In the year A.D. 66 they rose in revolt. The Romans were driven out and were only able to reconquer Judea after five years of hard fighting. Jerusalem fell after a terrible siege. The temple was burned to the ground. Thousands of Jews were slaughtered and many thousands more were exiled or sold into slavery. A few pockets of resistance remained. The last battle was fought in A.D. 73 at Masada, a desert rock fortress. After a fierce fight, 960 Jewish defenders took their own lives rather than be taken prisoner.

Sixty years later, a second Jewish revolt broke out against the Romans. It was led by Bar-Kochba. The Roman emperor, Hadrian, was forced to send almost 100,000 troops to restore order. The Romans built a new city on the ruins of Jerusalem, called Aelia Capitolina. The province was renamed Palaestina, after the Philistines, in place of Judea.

Jewish culture still thrived on the coast and later in Galilee. The city of Tiberias became a center of learning. Over 100 ancient places of worship, or synagogues, date from this period.

Over the ages, many Jews had been exiled or had settled abroad. These scattered Jewish communities were known as the Diaspora. Jews were living, working, and keeping their faith alive in many parts of Europe and Asia.

The cross and the crescent
Christianity only developed as a separate religion after the death of Jesus. At first, Christians were persecuted by the Romans. However, in 325, Emperor Constantine accepted Christianity as the official state religion of Rome. He moved the capital of the empire eastward from Rome to the city of Byzantium. He rebuilt this magnificent city, which was named Constantinople after him. Today, it is in Turkey and is known as Istanbul. This Christian empire was to last 1,000 years, but its rule of the Holy Land was to last for just 300 years. Many splendid churches, monasteries,

and towns were built during this period. Some still stand, such as the Church of the Nativity in Bethlehem.

In 570, the prophet Mohammed was born at Mecca, in Arabia. He preached a new faith called Islam, and soon had many followers, called Muslims. In 636 Muslim Arab armies invaded the Holy Land and Christian rule came to an end. The new faith, whose symbol was the crescent, eventually extended from Spain to India. These were glorious years for Islam. Many advances were made in areas such as medicine, science, and philosophy. Some outstanding examples of Islamic architecture of this period may still be seen today. The beautiful Dome of the Rock in Jerusalem is sacred to Muslims as the spot from which Mohammed rose to heaven.

Holy wars

Both Christians and Muslims believed that they had a religious duty to fight for the Holy Land. The Christians called such a holy war a crusade. The Muslims called it a *jihad*.

The Christian lands of Europe banded together to send armies to the Holy Land. The First Crusade arrived from Europe in 1099. It reached Jerusalem and massacred its population. Most other parts of the country soon fell too, and the Crusaders set up a kingdom with its capital at Jerusalem. Many of the Christian knights returned to Europe, but others stayed. They built towns and castles. However, in 1187 Saladin, the Kurdish-born ruler of Egypt and Syria, crushed the Christian armies at the Horns of Hattin, in Galilee. The Kingdom of Jerusalem fell apart, and

The Lower Galilee fortress of Belvoir (meaning "beautiful view") was one of the mightiest in the Crusader kingdom. After Saladin's victory over the Crusaders in 1187, Belvoir alone remained undefeated.

the Christians were driven out of the area.

In 1191, a new crusade was assembled in Europe to reclaim the Holy Land. It was led by King Richard I of England, known as Coeur de Lion or Lionheart, and the French King Philip II. The Christians won back part of the Holy Land, but failed to take Jerusalem. The new capital was the port of Acre, on the coast. By the middle of the thirteenth century the Muslims again had the Crusaders on the retreat. The Muslim leader was Baybars, the Sultan of the Egyptian Mameluke empire. The Christians sailed for Europe in 1291. Their fortresses were destroyed and parts of the Coastal Plain were flooded to prevent a return.

The Ottoman Turkish empire

In 1516 the Ottoman Turks, who were also Muslims, conquered much of the Middle East, including Israel, from the Mamelukes. Israel was divided into districts, each with a Turkish governor. Apart from collecting the heavy taxes, the governors usually had little interest in the local population of Muslim Arabs, Christians, and Jews. The neglect of farmland, the poverty, and the lack of law and order made Israel a hard place to live in during this period.

There were several rebellions against the Turks by local governors, and even foreign invasions like that of Napoleon Bonaparte in 1799, and the Egyptians in 1831. These sometimes brought the people relief from the hard Turkish rule. European Jews emigrated to Israel throughout the Turkish period, and many Arabs migrated into the country from nearby Syria and Arabia.

In the nineteenth century the situation began to improve. The new immigrants, investments from abroad, an improvement in transportation, and new inventions like the steam engine all helped the economy. As the Ottoman empire grew weaker, European powers like Great Britain, France, and Russia competed for control of the Holy Land. One reason was the special meaning the Christian holy places had for them. The more important reason for their interest, however, was the strategic position of Israel as a gateway to the region, and to the Far East. The defeat of the Ottoman empire in World War I brought Israel, now called Palestine, under British control.

4   A New State

A British force entered Palestine in 1916, as part of the struggle against the Ottoman empire. They assisted the Arabs of Palestine, who revolted against Turkish rule in the hope of achieving independence after the war. In 1917, British troops from Egypt broke through the Turkish defenses and captured Jerusalem.

Many Jews hoped that a new homeland for the Jews could be founded in Palestine. Small groups of Jews from Eastern Europe had begun to settle in Palestine from 1882 onward. They believed in the ideas of Zionism. In 1917, the British foreign secretary, Lord Balfour, declared that "His Majesty's Government views with favour the establishment in Palestine of a Jewish national home." World War I ended in 1918, and an international League of Nations was formed in 1919. It gave Great Britain the "mandate" or responsibility for the administration of Palestine. The text of the mandate included the actual words of the Balfour declaration. A Jewish state was to be created in Palestine for the first time in hundreds of years.

The proposal was bitterly resisted by the Arabs of Palestine, who themselves had lived in the region for many centuries. They wished to create an independent Arab state and objected to further Jewish immigration. During the 1920s and 1930s the Arabs fought with Jewish settlers. By 1936, about 250,000 Jews had returned to settle the land. In this year the Arabs revolted against the British, declaring the mandate to be unjust.

Many small Jewish settlements in the 1930s were built in just a single day. In 1939, with special concern for security, the prefabricated tower and stockade walls of Dafna in Upper Galilee are erected while a tractor breaks ground for the first crop.

What Is Zionism?

Zion is one of the ancient Biblical names for Jerusalem. For thousands of years Jews everywhere in the world faced Jerusalem in prayer. They prayed to return to the land of their ancestors. Over the centuries, many did return. Theodor Herzl (1860–1904) was a European Jew who was born in Budapest. He became leader of a political movement called Zionism. The First World Zionist Congress was held in 1897.

Zionism is based on the understanding that although Jews had been scattered over the ages, they remained a people, and not just a religious group. Zionists felt that they had a special right to return to their ancient homeland. They aimed to help Jews settle in Palestine and to work toward the creation of a Jewish state there. The Zionists were opposed by the Arabs already living in Palestine.

War and mass murder

During the 1930s, many Jews living in Germany were persecuted and terrorized by members of a political group called the Nazis. The leader of the Nazis was Adolf Hitler. The Nazis came to power in Germany in 1933. They took over, or annexed, Austria in 1938 and ordered the invasion of neighboring countries such as Czechoslovakia.

In 1939, World War II broke out in Europe. The Allied forces eventually included the United States, Britain, Canada, India, Australia and New Zealand, South Africa, and the Soviet Union. They fought Germany, Italy, and Japan. When the Germans were finally defeated in 1945, the world was horrified to discover that the Nazis had brutally murdered millions of people, among

In the 1930s and 1940s about 100,000 Jewish refugees from Nazi Europe tried to reach Palestine, most in old, overcrowded ships. The most famous was the Mississippi River steamer, renamed Exodus 1947, *which tried to beat the British naval blockade with 4,500 immigrants on board.*

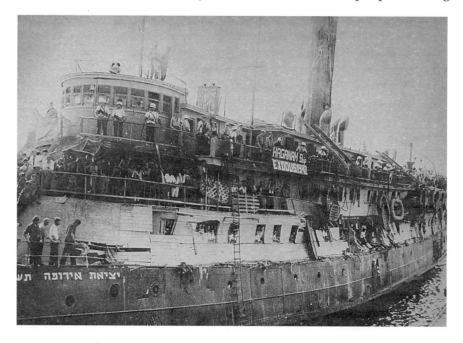

them six million Jews. Two-thirds of the Jewish population of Europe had been gassed or starved to death in terrible camps. This tragedy became known as the Holocaust. Jews were more determined than ever to have their own country, where they could live in safety.

During World War II, many Palestinian Jews volunteered to join the Allied forces. Many more helped the war effort with industrial work. However, tension developed between the British government and the Jews in Palestine. The British limited Jewish immigration and restricted the purchase of land by settlers. Jewish underground organizations were formed, some of which were to use terrorist methods in the coming struggle.

The founding of Israel

After the war, Palestine was the scene of a bitter three-way struggle between Jews, Arabs, and British. In 1945, the United Nations Organization was formed to replace the old League of Nations. In 1947, Britain disengaged itself from the struggle by informing the United Nations that it no longer wished to govern Palestine. The United Nations voted to approve the partition of Palestine. It was to be divided into two states, one for the Palestinian Arabs, and one for the Jews.

The Jews did not approve of much of the partition plan. However they decided to accept it, because they believed it was the best deal they could expect at the time. The Arabs rejected partition from the start. On May 14, 1948, Britain withdrew from Palestine. The Jews declared an independent state, to be known as Israel.

The next day, the forces of the neighboring

Arab states combined to attack Israel. Israel withstood the attack, but war continued until early 1949, when there was a ceasefire. By then, Israel had occupied some of the territory that the United Nations had intended as a state for the Palestinian Arabs. The Kingdom of *Transjordan*, today known as Jordan, had occupied the eastern part of Jerusalem and a large mountainous area to the north and south of the city, which became known as the West Bank. Egypt had captured a narrow piece of land along the Mediterranean coast, known as the Gaza Strip.

Israel was accepted as a member of the United Nations on May 11, 1949. Jews set about building their new state with enthusiasm.

Early years
The Arabs who remained in the new State of Israel became full citizens. However, thousands of Palestinian Arabs had lost their homes in the fighting. Refugees made their homes in wretched camps in the Gaza Strip and the West Bank. The Palestinian Arabs had no state of their own, and the seeds of future conflict remained.

A huge number of Jewish immigrants reached Israel in the first few years of the new state's existence. The Jewish population of 650,000 in 1948 doubled in three years. By 1958, it had trebled. The newcomers were Jews fleeing wartorn Europe, and from the Arab countries of North Africa and the Middle East. The 1950s were hard years for the new state, but new towns and settlements were founded. Agriculture and industry expanded. Education and welfare were provided for the rapidly growing population.

Israel at war

In 1964, the Palestine Liberation Organization (PLO) was founded. The PLO was a political and military organization whose original aim was the creation of a Palestinian Arab state to replace Israel. It included a number of groups, several of which made terrorist attacks on Israeli civilians during the following years, and clashed with Israeli troops. The PLO leader was named Yasser Arafat.

The State of Israel was not recognized by its neighbors. In 1967, the armies of Egypt, Jordan, and Syria fought against Israel in the Six-Day War. Israel resisted the attack and invaded new territory. Egypt lost the Gaza Strip and the huge Sinai Peninsula. Jordan lost East Jerusalem and the West Bank. Syria lost the Golan Heights in the north. Sinai has since been returned to Egypt. East Jerusalem was annexed, however, and the remaining territories are still under Israeli occupation.

In 1973, Israel was again attacked by Egypt and Syria in a short but bitter war. In 1977, the Egyptian President Anwar Sadat decided to try the way of peace. His courageous visit to Jerusalem began a process that resulted in the 1979 peace agreement between Israel and Egypt. However, 1982 saw further trouble to the north. PLO attacks from Lebanon on Israeli civilian targets increased. A strong military response by the Israeli defense forces developed into a major campaign in Lebanon, which lasted until 1985.

At the end of 1987, Arabs in the Occupied Territories began a long campaign of violence against Israeli troops and civilians, striking, throwing stones, and setting vehicles on fire. The Israeli troops reacted aggressively in this uprising, or *intifada*. Arab houses were demolished and many Arabs were killed.

In 1988, the PLO declared Palestine an independent, if stateless, nation. They agreed to give up terrorism and to recognize Israel's right to exist. Israel's chief ally, the United States, was now prepared to talk to the PLO, but the Israeli government was not. Israel wished to see the PLO call a halt in the intifada to show their genuine intent before they would negotiate.

Although the Israeli nation has existed for 40 years and desperately needs peace, few Israelis can agree on how it is to be achieved.

The State of Israel

How is Israel governed today? The State of Israel is a democratic republic. Every citizen over the age of 18 has the right to vote. The head of state is the president. This is not a political position. Like a British king or queen, the Israeli president receives new foreign diplomats and represents the nation at official ceremonies. The president is elected for a five-year term by the members of the Knesset, Israel's parliament, and cannot serve more than two terms.

Politics and parties

The Knesset, Israel's parliament, is responsible for passing the laws by which Israel is governed. It has only one "house," unlike the two of the United States Congress or the British Parliament. There are 120 seats. In addition to its general sessions, it has ten different committees made up

The General Session Hall of the Knesset. The seats are arranged in the form of the "menorah" (candelabra), the state symbol. Addressing the Knesset on this historic occasion, in November 1977, is the Egyptian president Anwar Sadat.

of Knesset members. Each committee is responsible for a subject like foreign affairs and security, economics, or education and culture. The committee debates new laws and works out how they are to be worded before the full Knesset votes on them.

The two main political parties in Israel are called Likud and Labor. There are many smaller parties representing religious and other interests. In the Knesset elections of November 1988, 27 parties competed. Fifteen of them won seats.

The system of elections is a type known as proportional representation. Before an election, each party publishes its list of candidates in an order fixed by the party itself. The country is not divided into voting districts, and candidates do not represent a particular area.

The votes throughout the country are added up. A party has to get at least one percent of all the votes cast nationwide to get a seat in the Knesset. The 120 seats are then divided up among the successful parties on a proportional basis. If a certain party gets 10 percent of all the votes cast, it will be awarded 10 percent of the Knesset seats, that is, 12 seats.

This system makes it hard for one party alone to get a majority in the Knesset. Governments in Israel are usually coalitions, or partnerships of various parties. Once the results of an election are known, the president invites the leaders of each successful party to meet him in turn. Each party informs the president whom it would support to head the new government and become prime minister. The president then lets the leader who seems to have the most support try to form a government. This system results in small parties having a great deal of power in Israel, because the large parties depend on their support to form a government. Many Israelis are campaigning to reform the system of elections.

The laws of the land
Many countries, such as the United States, have a written constitution that defines the way in which they are to be governed. Israel, like Great Britain, has none, but it does have several laws that were designed to be part of such a document at a future date. These are known as the Basic Laws. They deal with the Knesset, the government, the presidency, and territorial questions.

Proposed laws that have been drafted by committee are presented to the Knesset in the form of a bill. If the bill is passed, it becomes law. A few old laws still date from the days of the Ottoman empire and the British mandate. Some laws dealing with personal matters such as marriage, divorce, and inheritance are based upon the religious traditions of the various communities living in Israel. Such laws are enforced by separate religious courts.

Israel has local city and magistrates' courts, more important regional courts, and a Supreme Court that is the highest in the land. The Supreme Court often sits as a High Court of Justice, which may hear appeals at very short notice and issue orders accordingly. Israel has no jury system, but the accused may be tried by a panel of three, five, or even more judges.

Armed forces

Israel's history has been one of constant strife, and today almost one-third of Israel's national budget is spent on defense. Army, navy, and air force are part of a single organization called the Israeli Defense Force (IDF). All Jewish and Druze (see page 57) men must serve for three years in the IDF from the age of 18 and will later serve as part-time reserves. Unmarried Jewish women must serve two years in the IDF, although they may be exempted on military grounds. Arab citizens are not drafted into the IDF but may volunteer.

5 Peoples, Languages, and Faiths

However beautiful a country is, and however interesting its history, it is the people who live in it who really determine its character. The people of Israel today come from a variety of backgrounds, each with its religious and cultural differences. Each has its own shrines, holidays, and colorful ceremonies. These have been added to by the fact that Jewish immigrants have come from over 100 countries. More than one-third of the population was born outside Israel. They have brought with them their languages, their customs, their folklore, and their foods.

The Hebrew language
Hebrew is the first language of about 3 million Jewish Israelis, and is the official language of the State of Israel. It has been developed from the language spoken by Jews more than 3,000 years ago, in which the Jewish Bible, or the Old Testament, was written. Hebrew was still spoken 2,000 years ago, but by then another, related language called Aramaic was more widely spoken. Written Hebrew adopted the Aramaic script, which is still used today.

When the Romans destroyed Jewish independence, the Jews were scattered over many lands. Hebrew survived as their common language, but it was used only for prayers, religious works, and poetry. It was not a living language that developed and changed. Jews

Jerusalem under snow, looking from Mount of Olives. The magnificent gold Dome of the Rock is a Muslim shrine, built on the site of the ancient Jewish Temple. To the left and behind the Dome is the large gray dome of the Holy Sepulcher, where Jesus died and was buried.

English	Hebrew	Arabic
hello	Shalom	Marhaba
please	berakasha	iza samachat
thank you	todah	shookran
my name is ...	shmee ...	ana ismee ...
		(boy)
		ana ismeek ...
		(girl)
What's your name?	ma shimcha?	shu ismak?
	(to a male)	(to a male)
	ma shmeich?	shu ismeek?
	(to a female)	(to a female)
I live in ...	ani gar be ...(boy)	ana suken be ...
		(boy)
	ani gara be ...(girl)	ana sukne be ...
		(girl)

49

spoke the languages of the countries in which they lived. Some new languages developed. One was Ladino, a mixture of Hebrew and Spanish. Another was Yiddish, a dialect of German mixed with Hebrew and Slavic words, but written in the Hebrew script. This was spoken mainly in Central and Eastern Europe.

The revival of Hebrew as a modern spoken language was almost entirely due to one man. His name was Eliezer Ben-Yehuda. He arrived in Israel from Europe in 1881. His passion for speaking only Hebrew ran into opposition from religious Jews. They thought that Hebrew was a "holy tongue" not suitable for everyday use. However, Ben-Yehuda went ahead, creating new words out of ancient ones to meet the necessities of a modern world. His son became the first modern child to speak Hebrew as his natural language.

Other languages

Arabic is also an official language in Israel. It is spoken by about 700,000 Arabs and 50,000 Druzes, who have lived in what is now northern Israel for hundreds of years. It is the language of instruction in their schools. It is the most common language of the Middle East and North Africa. Government publications are produced in both Hebrew and Arabic, and the Knesset may be addressed by members in either language.

Many immigrants still use the language of the country they come from, whether it is English (the most common), French, German, Yiddish, Russian, or Ladino. It is estimated that Jews in Israel speak almost 100 languages!

What Is a Sabra?
An Israeli Jew born in Israel is known as a sabra. The *sabra* is the edible prickly pear, a cactus common in Israel. They say that the locals are like that, a bit prickly on the outside, but sweet on the inside.

The Jewish community

The Jewish community in Israel today numbers over 3.5 million people. Many are of Ashkenazi cultural background. This means that their families once lived in countries of Central or Eastern Europe, such as Germany, Poland, Russia, or Hungary. Many others, however, are Sephardic. Their ancestors were expelled from Spain (*Sepharad* in the Hebrew language) in 1492. Jews who came more recently from countries such as Morocco, Algeria, Syria, or Turkey are generally from this group. Some Jews also came to Israel from India, Yemen, and Ethiopia, these are often grouped with the Sephardic Jews.

The Jewish faith

The Jewish religion is known as Judaism. Its traditional form is said to be "orthodox." It traces its roots back to the relationship believed to have existed between the patriarch Abraham and

A Land of Many Faiths
* 82 percent follow the Jewish faith
* 14 percent are Muslim
* 2.3 percent are Christian
* 1.7 percent are Druzes

Jews gather every day to worship at the Western or Wailing Wall. This is the outer wall of the Temple Mount. Jewish religious tradition forbids entering the area of the destroyed Temple (now the Muslim Dome of the Rock), and the Wall developed as a holy place instead. The largest of the 2,000-year-old stones weighs 400 tons.

God, as described in the Bible. The Ten Commandments, said to have been given to Moses by God, form the basis of the Laws of Moses, which are found in the Torah. Thousands of years later, Jewish scholars called rabbis interpreted the laws of the Torah for day-to-day practical use. These teachings were passed down by word of mouth from one generation to the next. Eventually they were written down in the many books known as the Talmud.

About 20 percent of Israeli Jews would call themselves "religious," and try to observe the regulations of the Talmud. Many others might say they are "traditional," and keep some of the

Jewish Festivals

Rosh Hashanah, the Jewish New Year, falls in September. **Yom Kippur,** the Day of Atonement, comes ten days later. It is the most sacred day of the year, when Jews ask God to forgive their sins of the past year.

On **Sukkot,** or Tabernacles, in October, many Jews build little shelters of branches to recall the living conditions of the ancient Israelites during their years in the desert.

Passover, in the spring, is celebrated with an elaborate family meal called the *seder.* Special foods are eaten, like the unleavened *matza* bread. Songs, stories, and prayers recall how the Israelites were saved from slavery in Egypt 3,300 years ago.

Seven weeks later comes the harvest festival of **Shavuot,** which also commemorates Moses receiving the Law from God.

Other national holidays include **Purim,** a merry spring festival of fancy dress and fun. **Chanukah,** in December, is a Festival of Lights. Candles are lit each evening for eight days, to commemorate the revolt of the Maccabees 22 centuries ago.

May sees three important festivals for modern Israel. There is the sombre **Holocaust Memorial Day,** for the six million Jewish victims of the Nazis in World War II. There is the **Day of Remembrance** for the nation's fallen soldiers. Finally, there is the celebration of Israel's **Day of Independence.**

customs of the Sabbath and holy days. Since Jewish festivals are national holidays, and school Bible studies are in the original Hebrew, it is not difficult for Jews to feel Jewish in Israel, even if they do not go to synagogue.

A good number of the most devout Jews belong to a group called *Hassidim*, which means "pious ones." The men have beards, and wear long black coats, black hats, and often stockings with knickerbockers below their knees. The women dress extremely modestly. Married women keep their hair covered with a tight scarf or a wig. They do not ignore the modern world, but reject many of its values. They have nothing to do with television, sports, or entertainment.

Jews believe that they have a special religious tie to the land of Israel, and this belief inspired them to create the modern State of Israel.

The Muslim community

Well over half of Israel's 600,000 Muslims live in urban areas. These include large cities like

Muslim Festivals
The Muslim calendar, like the Jewish one, goes by the moon. Unlike the Jewish calendar, it has no leap years, so festivals fall 10 or 11 days earlier each year. The end result is that they can be celebrated in any season.

The **Feast of the Sacrifice** is known as the Great Festival, and falls in the twelfth month of the Muslim calendar. Throughout the month of **Ramadan** Muslims neither eat nor drink from sunrise to sunset. The month of fasting ends with a three-day festival called **Id al-fitr,** or the Small Festival.

A Druze farmer dressed in traditional baggy trousers comes home from his fields with his simple wooden plow. The turban on his head indicates he is one of the religious leaders of his community.

Nazareth, Haifa, Jaffa, and Jerusalem, and many smaller towns. The rest live in rural villages, especially in the Galilee hills, and farm or commute into nearby towns for work.

Most of Israel's Arabs belong to the main sect of Islam, which is known as Sunni. The minarets, or towers, of their mosques are landmarks in every town and village. The life of many Arabs is organized around the prayer times, which form an important part of a Muslim's day. In the cities, however, religion tends to play a less important part in the lives of many Arabs.

Hospitality still forms an important part of the Arab way of life. A host who is able to provide refreshments and coffee for large numbers of

Robed Roman Catholic monks in procession to the Church of the Nativity in Bethlehem on the afternoon before Christmas. The church is 1,400 years old and is shared by Roman Catholic, Greek Orthodox, and Armenian Orthodox. Note the different crosses above the church.

guests gains respect in the community. Often, the largest and busiest living room in a village is that of the *mukhtar*, or headman. Here, village elders may gather to discuss community affairs.

Islam and the Koran
Islam, the religion of the Muslims, was founded by the Prophet Mohammed about 1,350 years ago. *Islam* means submission to the will of God, or

Allah, as revealed in the holy book of the Koran. The essentials of Muslim belief are known as the Five Pillars of Islam. Muslims must declare that "There is no God but Allah, and Mohammed is his prophet." They must pray facing their holy city of Mecca, which is in Saudi Arabia, five times a day. They must fast, or not eat, from sunrise to sunset during the Islamic month of Ramadan. They must give to charity and go on pilgrimage to Mecca. The Muslim sabbath is on Friday.

The Druze and their faith
The Druze religion broke away from Islam about 1,000 years ago. It became a completely different faith. The Druzes keep details of their religion secret. Even within their own community, only one person in 20 shares the secret. There is little public religious life, except for celebrations such as that honoring Jethro. Jethro was Moses's father-in-law, whom the Druzes believe to have been a great prophet.

There are over 50,000 Druzes in Israel. Many live in two very big villages on Mount Carmel, near Haifa. There are also four Druze villages in the Occupied Territories, on the Golan Heights. The 6,000 inhabitants of these villages remain citizens of Syria. There are other Druze communities in Syria and in Lebanon.

Traditionally a mountain people, the Druzes live by herding and farming. The older Druze men usually sport walrus-style moustaches and some wear black, baggy trousers. Druze women play a more active role in society than is common in the Middle East. Druzes speak Arabic, but do not consider themselves Arabs.

The Christian community

There are 103,000 Christians in Israel. A few thousand of these are Europeans or other westerners, many of whom are clergy serving in local parish churches or in monasteries. Jerusalem and Galilee are holy places to Christians and the clergy serve thousands of visiting Christians every year. All the others are Arabs, whose ancestors became Christians many centuries ago. Most live in towns, although there are a few Galilee villages with Christian communities.

The New Testament is the source of faith for Christians. Its first four books are called the Gospels, which means "good news." Christians believe that Jesus was the Messiah sent by God, and that he was actually the divine Son of God. They believe that Jesus deliberately gave his life on the cross to pay for the sins of the world. They believe that after his crucifixion he came back to life and ascended to heaven. Christians wait for Jesus to return and fulfill his promise of a Kingdom of God. The Christian sabbath is on Sunday.

The Bedouin

The Bedouin are made up of nomadic tribes who move from place to place with their tents, their camels, and their flocks of sheep and goats. Most of the 50,000 Bedouin who live in Israel live in the Negev Desert. They follow the Islamic faith. The traditional Bedouin way of life is a daily battle against the harsh desert environment, with its burning sands and lack of water. The patriarchs of the Bible must have followed much the same pattern of existence thousands of years ago.

Times have changed, however. Today, many Bedouin have settled down in permanent encampments of tents, shacks, or even modern houses. Some farm a little, and some find work in the nearby towns. Even in the more traditional encampments, the aerials of television sets operated by a generator poke out of many goat-hair tents.

The Bahai

The Bahai faith was founded in what is now Iran, in the nineteenth century. The Bahai believe that people throughout the world will one day be united and that the difference between religions will eventually disappear. The world center of the faith is in Haifa, where there is the magnificent tomb of the Bab, the martyr who foretold the coming of the prophet Baha'ullah. The tomb of Baha'ullah, Bahai's holiest shrine, is in Acre. Although there is only a tiny Bahai community in Israel, there are Bahais throughout the world.

6   Living in Israel

Most Israelis are city dwellers, living in the built-up areas of Jerusalem, greater Tel Aviv, and Haifa. In general, people buy their own apartments. There is little rental housing. Single-family houses are unusual within the cities, but are more common in the suburbs.

Life in Jerusalem
Jerusalem is a city built upon hills. These offer many fine views of the city and its surroundings. Most buildings are built out of the honey-colored local limestone. The ancient sites and religious shrines, especially in and around the walled Old City, give Jerusalem a character that is unique in the world. Large numbers of Orthodox Jews have made their homes in Jerusalem. The religious feeling is palpable on Friday night, the eve of the

---

Where Do Israelis Live?

★ Two-thirds of all Israelis live on the Coastal Plain.

★ The largest cities are Jerusalem (population 483,000), Tel Aviv–Jaffa (population 320,000), and Haifa (population 224,000).

★ The largest urban area is that of greater Tel Aviv, which has a total population of about 1,650,000. Three out of eight Israelis live in this area.

★ Three percent of all Israelis live on the communal settlements call *kibbutzim*.

★ Just over three percent live in cooperative villages called *moshavim*.

Jewish holy day or Sabbath. The whole city center is shut down, and people entertain in their homes or visit friends.

City centers

In contrast to Jerusalem, Tel Aviv comes to life on Sabbath eve. Its restaurants and nightspots are packed. For many, a nice weekend is the time to head for the beaches of the Mediterranean coast. Tel Aviv was only founded in 1909, but it has grown to merge with the much older town of Jaffa. The city is the country's most important business center, and is near Ben Gurion International Airport. Tel Aviv's hotels serve tourists and business people from all over the world.

Many people think that Haifa is Israel's loveliest city. It is built on the slopes of Mount

Tel Aviv's beautiful Mediterranean beach with Old Jaffa in the background. The city is Israel's commercial center. Its lively character and mild climate has also made Tel Aviv the center of entertainment and leisure-time activity.

The Holy City
Jerusalem is one of the most remarkable cities in the world. It is regarded as holy by three of the world's great religions.

To Jews, it is the national capital and the center of their religion. For 3,000 years Jews have turned to Jerusalem when they pray. Jerusalem was the site of the Temple, but all that remains of the Second Temple, destroyed by the Romans, is the Western Wall of its plaza. Many Jews gather to worship at the Wall, called the Wailing Wall, every day.

Christians regard Jerusalem as holy because so many important events in the life of Jesus took place in the city. For some Christians, Jerusalem has become the symbol of the perfect city of God in the future, which they call the New Jerusalem.

Jerusalem is the third holiest city of Islam, after Mecca and Medina in Saudi Arabia. Muslims believe that the Prophet Mohammed rose to heaven from here, to receive God's word. The site is marked by the Dome of the Rock.

Carmel, amid pine trees and parks. It looks out over Haifa Bay and its harbor. The city is livelier than Jerusalem, but smaller and quieter than Tel Aviv. It is a favorite port of call for ships on Mediterranean cruises.

Eilat, with a population of only 25,000, is small even by Israeli standards. In 1949, it was nothing more than a tiny police post with a mud hut, called Umm Rush-Rush. Since then it has been developed into a tourist resort. It lies between spectacular red and gray mountains and the blue, crystal-clear waters of the Red Sea.

New towns

The huge number of Jewish refugees that reached Israel after 1948 could not be absorbed by the existing cities, and not everyone wanted to be a farmer. The solution was to build settlements, known as "development towns." Most were brand new, but in some cases existing small towns were expanded. Some, like Dimona and Arad in the Negev, were planned near a natural resource that could be developed to create jobs. Some new towns grew as economic needs developed, like Ashdod with its large port and industrial area. Some became centers that provided services for a region. Others were built to improve security, near sensitive borders. Since 1967, numerous Jewish villages have sprung up in the Occupied Territories, often in places where Jews lived long ago. Many people object to these villages being built, because of rival claims to the areas.

What is a kibbutz?

A kibbutz is a communal or collective village. Israel has over 250 kibbutzim. The members of the community do not work for their own profit, but for the community as a whole. In return they get all they need from the kibbutz including housing, meals, education, full health care, vacations, and a personal allowance.

The earliest kibbutz was Degania, founded in 1909 by Jewish pioneer settlers from Eastern Europe. They wished to create a fair society where everyone would be equal, and people would help each other. Their motto was "From each according to his abilities, to each according

Kibbutz kindergarten children with garlands for the Shavuot harvest festival. Kibbutz children benefit from very small classes, a huge amount of outdoor space, and a strong feeling of security in their community.

to his needs." There were practical reasons for this way of life, as well as idealistic ones. It was easier for a group to clear swampy or rocky land for farming, and to defend the settlement against hostile neighbors.

The way a kibbutz runs its affairs is very democratic. All important decisions are taken by majority vote at the weekly general meeting of adult members. Day-to-day matters are taken care of by elected committees. A kibbutz normally has only a few hundred members. It is a close-knit society, so the community is careful about whom it accepts as a member. There is usually a one-year trial period, after which two-thirds of the kibbutz must vote to approve the new member.

Almost all kibbutzim make their income by

farming, but most have developed other businesses as well. These may include an electronics or plastics factory, a hotel or restaurant for tourists, or arts and crafts. Some members work outside the kibbutz as social workers or teachers, for example, but their salary is paid directly to the kibbutz.

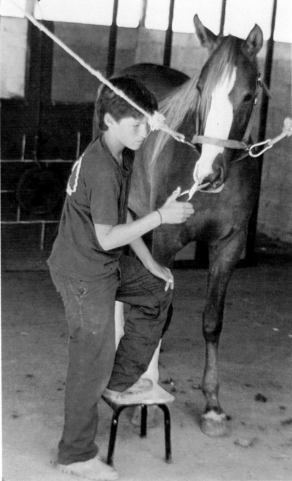

Everyone takes part in life on a kibbutz. After school this boy's responsibilities include grooming the horses. Breeding thoroughbred Arabian horses for export has become a small but profitable business in Israel.

The Moshav
A moshav (plural moshavim) is a cooperative farming village, usually made up of about 60 to 100 families. The first one was Nahalal in the Jezre'el Valley, set up in 1921.

The moshav movement became very popular in the 1950s. Large numbers of Jewish refugees from Arab countries wanted to settle on the land, but did not like the communal way of life on the kibbutz. On a moshav they could work independently for themselves, but still enjoy the mutual help and cooperation of a close community. Today, Israel has over 450 moshavim.

School days

Education is Israel is compulsory, and free from the age of five to 16. The vast majority of children go to nursery schools even before they turn five, and most remain in secondary school until they are 18. There are about 1.3 million children in Israeli schools. About 80 percent are Jewish, and their schools are run in Hebrew. Some 20 percent are Arab or Druze, and they study in Arabic.

The Jewish schools are divided into three main groups, or streams. Over 80 percent of them belong to the National stream. These offer a general education, including Jewish traditions and Bible studies. Schools in the National Religious stream give far more time to Jewish religious subjects, although general subjects are taught also. The smallest stream is the Independent, which is recognized by the government, but not supported by it. Children in these schools come from a group of very religious Jews known as the Ultra-Orthodox community. Except for the basic skills of reading, writing, and arithmetic, intensive religious studies make up the whole curriculum in these schools.

There are many vocational schools throughout Israel, where older pupils learn skills such as carpentry, metalwork, electronics, or cooking. At the same time they continue some of their general education. Agricultural schools offer training in farming. Both vocational and agricultural schools offer teaching in Hebrew and in Arabic.

There are also special schools for blind or deaf children, and for those with serious physical,

Schoolboys learn to make fine furniture at a vocational school in the Arab village of Kafr Kari, near Hadera.

learning, or emotional problems. As often as possible, however, such pupils are kept in ordinary schools. In poor areas there are many small institutions that are open outside school hours. These offer children from difficult home situations a place to have a hot meal, work quietly, or get help with their homework. The children are kept off the streets, and are given the chance to acquire skills such as training with computers.

Going to college
There are seven full universities in Israel. The largest are the Hebrew University of Jerusalem, which has about 17,000 students, and Tel Aviv University, which has about 19,000. Some universities award degrees in religious studies as well as the usual general courses. The Ben-Gurion University of the Negev has a Desert Research Institute.

Other colleges of higher education offer courses in music, dance, textiles and fashion, technology, and physical education. There are several teacher-training colleges and community colleges. Adult education is catered to at the Open University in Tel Aviv, which offers a great variety of courses. Large community centers offer all kinds of afternoon and evening classes for young people and adults.

Health and hospitals
At the beginning of this century, sanitation and health care in Palestine was very poor. Today, Israel has one of the highest standards of medicine and public health in the world. Killer diseases such as malaria no longer threaten the

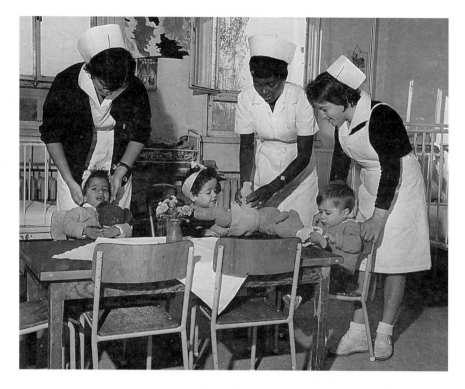

Nurses playing with children in a hospital ward. The African student is from Cameroon, doing advanced training in Israel.

region. Israel has led the way in some fields such as eye problems and bone diseases in children. There is one doctor for every 400 people in Israel, which is one of the best ratios in the world.

Israel is well equipped with general and specialist hospitals. Some are owned by the state or the city; others are run by private, religious, or charitable organizations. The tragic wars of Israel's recent history have given the country's medical system great experience in emergency medicine. Hospitals have developed advanced techniques for dealing with severe burns and injuries. Expert Israeli teams have always been

69

quick to fly anywhere in the world to help in the event of disasters such as earthquakes.

Most Israelis belong to one of four medical insurance plans. The largest of these, *Kupat Holim Kelalit*, is run by the Israeli *Histadrut* or General Labor Federation. Members of the plan pay into a fund that then pays for their treatment if they become sick.

The Israeli equivalent of the Red Cross is called *Magen David Adom*. It provides ambulance, first aid, and blood-bank services. Mother-and-child centers all over the country help with vaccinations and child-care advice.

Care in the community

Israel's system of social security and welfare services is based on the idea that a community should care for all its members. Social work offices throughout the country offer advice and help to people with social or financial problems. People are encouraged not to wait until a problem has become serious, however. Young people are given training and assistance so that they will be able to support themselves in society. A special telephone hotline in ten major cities allows young people to call in without giving their names, and get advice from specially trained counselors on any problem they have.

The National Insurance Institute provides money for pensions for the elderly, compensation for injuries that occur at work, unemployment benefits, hospital expenses for childbirth, and children's benefits. The funds to pay for these services are raised by a national insurance tax, which all Israelis must pay in addition to their regular income tax.

The labor movement

Israel's founders in 1948 were socialists, for whom the welfare of the country's workers was very important. Protecting the rights of the workers was mainly the job of the Histadrut, the General Labor Federation, which had been founded as early as 1920. It dealt with issues such as work hours, days of rest, payments for dismissed workers, equal pay for men and women, and the arbitration of work disputes.

The nature of the State of Israel has changed a great deal since 1948. However, the Histadrut is still a very powerful body. It represents the country's various trade unions in relations with the government and with employers. Strikes are only legal if they are first approved by the Histadrut. In the early days, Israeli workers often owned part of their companies and helped to run them. This has resulted in the unusual situation today in which the Histadrut itself owns many large firms, including a huge construction company and the biggest commercial bank in the nation.

7 Israel at Work

Israel is a small country, and the political strife of the last 40 years has posed many problems for its economy. Israel earns its living by farming and industry. It has few natural resources. Its central bank is called the Bank of Israel, and the unit of currency is the new shekel. Israel has 26 commercial banks, and many other firms offering financial services to industry and the public.

Dead Sea industries
Israel has few big deposits of metal or minerals. By far the most important resource is the great inland lake known as the Dead Sea. The lower reaches of the Jordan River and some other small streams drain into the Dead Sea. The lake has no outlet. Its waters evaporate, or dry, in the great heat. The minerals remaining in the water become very concentrated. If you take a glass of water from the Dead Sea and let it evaporate, you will be left with a third of a glass of pure minerals, part of which is our common salt. No plants or animals can live in such water, which is how the Dead Sea got its name.

The Dead Sea Works, which is responsible for extracting the minerals, has the slogan "The Dead Sea gives life!" This is because the main mineral extracted from the lake is potash, which is an important farm fertilizer. It is also used in the production of pesticides. The Dead Sea is also a source of large quantities of bromine, a liquid that has many industrial uses. It is used in the petroleum and chemical industries, in

At Sodom, the lowest place on Earth, canals feed Dead Sea water to evaporation ponds. The crystallized salts are separated and refined. A heap of potash ready to be shipped can be seen at the top of the picture.

photography, and in medicine. Magnesium and kitchen salts are also products of this amazing lake.

Mines and quarries

Copper has been mined for thousands of years near Eilat, at Timna, sometimes known as King Solomon's Mines. However, the modern mines closed down a few years ago, because a drop in world copper prices made them unprofitable.

Phosphates are mined in large quantities in the Negev Desert, especially near the Small Crater, not far from the town of Dimona. This mineral is

73

exported in the form of a white powder, and is used to manufacture high-grade fertilizers. Other minerals are mined in this area in small quantities. These include gypsum, used in making cement, fine quality clay for ceramics, and sand for making glass.

Limestone is quarried in many parts of Israel. Some of it, such as the famous Jerusalem stone, is used as a building material. Some is crushed to make lime for cement works.

Oil and coal

Every country needs energy resources to produce power and fuel. Israel has very few. It has very little oil and natural gas and no coal. There are no rivers big enough to produce hydroelectric energy, harnessing the power of running water. Israel has not yet decided to build any nuclear power stations.

The result is that Israel is forced to import 97 percent of its energy needs. In the past, this meant only oil. Today, over half of the country's electricity is produced by coal-fired power stations. A kind of rock called oil shale has been found in the Negev Desert. A certain amount of oil can be extracted from this, which may help a little in the future. Oil is still needed, of course, for transportation and industry as well as for power stations. There are refineries to turn imported crude oil into usable fuels at Haifa and Ashdod.

Power from the sun

What Israel does have in large quantities is sunshine. For this reason Israeli scientists have endeavored to find ways of using solar energy,

The parabolic mirror of this solar collector concentrates the sun's rays to produce heat. The heat produces energy needed to run an entire factory at Sha'ar Henegev in the Negev Desert.

the power of the sun. Power plants designed in Israel use large numbers of mirrors to concentrate the sun's rays and produce energy. Throughout the country there are water tanks and glass panels on roof-tops. Two-thirds of all Israeli homes get their hot water from solar heating.

Developing industry

There was almost no industry in Palestine and the Middle East until World War I. In the following

75

years industry developed greatly. It was mostly based on small factories and workshops, producing items like food, clothing, and household goods. Since 1948, a great industrial expansion has taken place in Israel. Some industries are based on local agriculture or mineral resources, like the food, textile, and certain chemical industries. Others were created because of the political situation, such as the petroleum and defense-related industries.

Some industries have been brought to Israel by its immigrants. At the beginning of World War II many Jewish diamond-cutters fled their homes in

A diamond-cutter works on a fast-spinning wheel, with the precious stone locked in a clamp. The wheel is coated with a mixture of oil and diamond dust, the only thing that will cut this super-hard gem.

Israel's first satellite, Ofek 1, heading for outer space. Israel Aircraft Industries, which developed both the satellite and the rocket system, produces a wide range of sophisticated aircraft and military equipment.

the Netherlands and Belgium when the Nazis invaded. Thanks to these refugees, Israel today is the world's top exporter of cut and polished diamonds. The rough stones are all imported, but the finished products earn over $2 billion every year.

Israeli industry has been supported by great advances in scientific and technological research. Although Israel is not a rich country, it spends over two percent of the country's income on research and development. Israel leads research in electronics, computers, scientific and medical instruments, lasers, and heavy engineering equipment.

77

Foreign trade

Israel trades with many countries around the world. Its main exports are diamonds, chemicals and oil products, citrus and vegetables, machinery, and manufactured goods. One-third of these exports go to the United States, one-third to countries of the European Economic Community, and one-third to the rest of the world. The main imports are oil and coal, wheat and other grains, vehicles, and household appliances. Nearly two-thirds of imports come from Europe.

Israel imports more than it exports, and so has a problem with its balance of trade. This has been helped by favorable trade agreements with the United States and Europe, and by the opening of new markets in Eastern Europe and Asia.

A group of American travel agents are guided through the narrow lanes of Safed. The old synagogues, artists' quarter, and clear mountain air make this picturesque town one of the popular tourist attractions of Upper Galilee.

The tourist industry

Over 1.5 million tourists visit Israel every year. Traditionally, many tourists have been Christian pilgrims, visiting the sites of the Holy Land, or Jews coming to see the new country or their relatives. Today, more and more tourists come simply to have a vacation and relax. Israel has over 300 sunny days a year. There are lovely white beaches and tropical coral reefs. Visitors can try water sports, skiing, horseback riding, or hiking. There are ancient sites to be seen, interesting museums, friendly people, and good food.

Tourists come from about 60 countries, including the United States, Britain, Canada, Germany, and France. Tourism is one of Israel's most profitable industries.

Transportation

Israeli industry is helped by the small size of the country, which means that transportation is no great problem. It takes less than an hour to drive from Jerusalem to Tel Aviv, and no more than seven hours to drive the length of the country from north to south. Most goods and bulk products, like potash or fuels, are moved by road to the ports. The Mediterranean ports of Haifa and Ashdod are Israel's link to the Americas and Europe, while Eilat on the Red Sea serves the trade with the Far East.

The public makes use of good bus services between towns and villages, or takes a large, shared taxi known as a *sherut*. Passenger trains are less important. The main rail route runs along the coast between Tel Aviv and Haifa. Internal air travel is mostly between Tel Aviv and Eilat, with some flights stopping at Jerusalem on the way. Only small aircraft fly to other areas such as Haifa or Upper Galilee.

Israel's international links include shipping from the ports of Ashdod, Haifa, and Eilat, and road connections with Cairo, the Egyptian capital. Bridges across the Jordan River link Israel with Jordan, but Israeli citizens are not permitted to travel by these routes. Israel's main link with the outside world is by air. Freight, including flowers and fruit for export, and a large amount of passenger traffic, passes through Ben Gurion International Airport near Tel Aviv.

Growing for market

Israel produces 95 percent of its own food, and exports many more food products than it im-

A farmer on a moshav tends his long-stem roses. Within 24 hours of cutting, these flowers will be for sale in the major cities of Europe.

Date palms on a kibbutz near the Sea of Galilee. Advanced techniques in Israel now produce a yield per tree five to ten times higher than in many other parts of the Middle East.

ports. Until recently it was a land of rocky soil, desert, swamps, and poor water resources. Successful agriculture was made possible by the work of the first Jewish settlers in clearing the land, and by the research of modern scientists.

Israel grows many kinds of flowers for export, including roses and carnations. It even sends tulips to the Netherlands during the months when the famous Dutch bulb fields are under snow. Crops such as tomatoes, cucumbers, peppers, and melons do very well.

Citrus cultivation is the most important kind of farming in Israel. The main crop is oranges, but grapefruit, lemons, tangerines, and pomeloes are also grown in quantity. Each year 1.5 million tons of citrus fruits are produced. More than one-third of that is exported, either as fruit or as processed juice. Other popular produce includes avocados, dates, bananas, apples, and peaches. Nuts such as almond, pecan, and pistachio are grown, mostly for the local market. Fine grapes are cultivated, both for eating and for making wine.

Field crops

Israel grows much of its own wheat, barley, and corn, but it still needs to import some from abroad. Rice, sugar, and feed-grains for livestock must also be imported. Cotton has been a very successful crop in Israel. Some Galilee kibbutzim claim to produce some of the highest yields per acre in the world. All cotton picking is done by huge machines. Other successful crops include peanuts, watermelons, potatoes, carrots, and

Winter melons for export grow on the world's lowest farm, in the bare desert just south of the Dead Sea. The wonderful sweet flavor of this off-season field crop has been famous in Israel itself for years.

sunflowers, the seed of which is turned into an edible oil. Chickpeas are grown to make the popular snacks of *felafel* and *hummus* salad.

Cattle, poultry, and fish

Israel's dairy farmers provide all the milk and milk products the country needs. The cows in Israel give a world-record, nationwide average of 6 gallons of milk per cow each day. Top milkers give double that amount. The dairy herds do not graze in open fields. They are kept in sheds and enclosures, where they are fed.

Good quality but small beef-cattle herds provide the country's fresh meat, although frozen beef is imported as well. Very large numbers of chickens and turkeys are raised, which many Israelis prefer to the more expensive red meat. Fish farms provide another source of food. Carp, St. Peter's fish, and other freshwater species are raised in ponds. A new technique developed in Eilat allows saltwater fish to be bred in cages in the ocean.

Making the desert bloom

Israeli scientists have discovered that, with a little imagination, the hot and dry desert can produce excellent crops. Some crops, like dates, need the heat. Others, like the jojoba bean, which produces a fine oil used in industry, are actually desert plants. Most important, however, is that the heat of the desert allows farmers to grow summer crops like tomatoes and melons in the winter! Large quantities of these top-grade products are exported every year. Irrigation of crops has become a fine art. The "drip" irrigation

At Avdat in the Negev, Hebrew University professor Even-Ari has reused ancient canals, dams, and farming techniques to trap run-off rainwater and create an efficient desert farm. His excellent wheat, grapes, olives, pistachios, apricots, and other crops are the result. On the ridge are the ruins of the ancient Nabatean and later a Byzantine town that developed these methods.

system was invented in Israel. Thin, plastic pipelines are laid on the ground, with small feeder holes near the roots of each plant or tree. Water and fertilizer trickle out only where needed, in amounts controlled by the farmer. Another method of irrigation is now being tested that makes use of trapped rainwater. This technique of irrigation was first used by people in the Negev Desert 2,000 years ago.

Scientists are always searching for water deep under the desert. Sometimes the water found is too brackish, or salty, for ordinary use. However, scientists have developed new varieties of crops such as tomatoes which can grow well on water of poor quality.

8   Arts and Leisure

Most Israelis like to surround themselves with their friends, and enjoy good company. On weekends they may go for a family picnic in the woods, a nature hike, a backyard barbecue, or a soccer match.

The weekend in Israel is short, beginning on Friday afternoon and continuing only through Saturday. Sunday is an ordinary workday. Religious Jews will not travel, play sports, or go for an outing on a Saturday, the Jewish Sabbath. However, everyone likes to socialize with their family or to enjoy a meal with their friends.

Eating Israeli-style

Israel has become home to people from many countries. These immigrants brought with them their own special traditions, including different styles of cooking. Yemenites, Moroccans, Persians, Italians, French, Russians, Indians, Argentinians, Vietnamese, and Americans are just some of the influences. Restaurants of every kind have opened up in every city. Once upon a time many of these restaurants would have been mainly for foreign tourists, but the Israelis themselves have caught on to the idea of eating out as a nice way to spend an evening.

Many people think of "Israeli food" as the Arab-style cooking found everywhere in the Middle East. There is some truth in this. A typical meal will include hummus (a sort of paste made of chickpeas), tahini (a thick sauce made from sesame seeds), eggplant served in various ways, and any number of salads based on the country's excellent fresh vegetables. Lamb dishes like shishkebab and chops are the traditional main courses, often served with rice. Turkish coffee and a sweet confection called baklava end the meal well. The cook's own background may result in many variations of this kind of meal. The traditional Eastern European Jewish dishes like chopped liver, chicken soup, or meat-stuffed pastry are also easy to find in Israel.

In the last few years restaurants specializing in vegetable pies, soups and salads, and sometimes fish have become very popular. Still, even the vegetables and wonderful milk products have not replaced chicken and meat as a major part of the eating habits of most Israelis.

It may not be easy to say exactly what Israeli food is like, but one thing is certain—it is not boring! As Israelis will say in Hebrew to wish you a hearty appetite, *Beteyaron!*

Arts and crafts

Many painters and sculptors live in Israel, but a small and far from wealthy country cannot provide a large market for works of art. Many artists sell their work to tourists, however, or exhibit their works abroad. The standard of Israeli jewelry and silverwork is particularly good, both in design and workmanship. Crafts such as weaving and pottery are also popular. Craft shows take place at Jaffa and in Jerusalem's Old City.

The concert-goers

Many Israelis are enthusiastic lovers of classical music. There are two full-sized orchestras, the

Jerusalem Symphony Orchestra and the world-famous Israel Philharmonic, which is based in Tel Aviv. Young musicians who show talent attend music academies in various cities. There is a Music Center for Youth in Jerusalem, and summer music camps are held all over Israel.

Jerusalem's huge Israel Festival is the summer showcase for both local and foreign musicians. Other annual festivals take place at the Kibbutzim Ein Gev and Kfar Blum, in Galilee, and on Kibbutz Shefayim in Acre. There is an international choral festival called the Zimriya every three years. Opera is popular, and the national company and foreign touring companies are well supported.

Israeli pop music is also alive and well. Groups

A teenage wind ensemble plays classical music under the trees of Kibbutz Ein Hashofet, near Mount Carmel. Every summer the kibbutz hosts workshops and a festival for talented young musicians.

and individual singers cover many of the rock and pop styles found in America and Europe, but some local bands are influenced by traditional Israeli folk music or by styles of other Middle Eastern countries. Visiting international stars draw huge crowds to Tel Aviv's Yarkon Park and Jerusalem's open-air Sultan's Pool.

Theater and dance

The theater is thriving in Israel, with many large and small companies playing to packed houses. There are children's theaters, puppet theaters, and street theater and mime.

There are about ten major dance groups in Israel. The best-known include the classical Israel Ballet, and the modern dance companies Bat

Sheva, Bat Dor, and the Kibbutz Dance Group. Inbal blends its dance techniques with those of folk dances, like those of the Yemenite Jews.

Radio and television

There are no privately owned radio and television stations in Israel. The state-owned Voice of Israel radio network operates five stations on both FM stereo and AM. Two have a mixture of music and general interest programs. One is a classical music station, and one broadcasts in Arabic. The fifth is a pop music station that also runs commercials.

Several times a day the Voice of Israel carries news and magazine programs in other languages, such as English, French, Spanish,

In 1987 the annual Israel Festival of the Performing Arts opened dramatically in Jerusalem. Famous Frenchman Philippe Petit crossed the deep Hinnom Valley on a tightrope. Ahead of him are the Old City walls.

Russian, and Yiddish. Israel broadcasts around the world, 22 hours a day in 18 languages.

Israel's only television station is also state-owned, but has considerable independence. There is only one regular channel, and a second experimental one. Daytime programming is prepared by the Educational Television network, and is geared to schoolchildren. Israel cinema has produced some excellent films over the years. However, a lack of money for training and for making new films has hit the industry hard.

A nation of readers

About 88 percent of Israelis can read and write. There are 160 book publishers putting out about 5,500 different new books each year. An annual Hebrew Book Week in the big cities draws huge crowds, and Jerusalem holds an International Book Fair every two years.

There are 20 daily newspapers in Israel, nine in Hebrew, and the rest in Arabic. In addition, 900 different magazines are published on almost every topic. About 600 of these are in Hebrew.

On the sports field

Many Israelis like to follow sports, but few actually take part themselves! Schools have PE instructors, but children do not have to take part in competitive sports, and there are few school sports leagues. On the other hand, there are 60 specialist sports schools in Israel, which train young people in ten different sports.

The most popular sport is soccer. Attendance at the games is poor, however, as most fans follow their teams by means of television, radio, and the press. Basketball has become a major sport in Israel and the top Israeli team, Maccabi Tel Aviv, won the European Championship both in 1977 and 1981.

Tennis has been the success story of the 1980s. A series of tennis centers was set up around the country. Within ten years, Israel had produced international tournament winners like Shlomo Glickstein and Amos Mansdorf.

There are active leagues for team sports like

Maccabi Tel Aviv captain Tal Brodie going for the winning basket over the head of an Italian player. Since 1977 this Israeli team has been one of the strongest in European basketball, and has twice won the European Championship.

A tense moment in the International Windsurfing Championship on the Mediterranean Sea off Nahariya. Israel has hosted the 420-class sailing championships as well.

volleyball and handball. Water sports like surfing and windsurfing are popular. Golfers have to make do with the country's only golf course, at Caeserea on the Mediterranean coast.

The Israeli sailing team was a particularly strong entry at the Seoul Olympics in 1988. Every four years the Maccabi Games are held in Israel, for Jewish athletes from around the world.

Israel's handicapped athletes are a major force in international competition. The national team brought home a large number of medals from the Seoul Olympics for the Handicapped in 1988.

9 The Future

In 1988, the State of Israel celebrated its fortieth birthday. It was a time for Israelis to take stock. What was in store for Israel in the future?

Many of the questions being asked are about internal politics. Does the system of election give too much power to the small political parties? Demands to change the system can certainly be expected in the future. Another area of debate concerns the constitution. Strong disagreements within Israel will probably prevent a written constitution from being drawn up in the near future.

There has been tension between religious Orthodox Jews and nonreligious and non-Orthodox Jews. Should movie theaters be open on the Sabbath? Should pig-farming still be illegal, because it offends the religious traditions of Orthodox Jews? Orthodox Jews today hold 18 seats in the Knesset, and this gives them a lot of power and influence.

Israel's economy

Recent years have been hard for Israel's economy. Tourism and other industries have suffered losses, and others are in financial trouble. Bad weather conditions have caused poor harvests and market prices have dropped.

However, some solutions have been found. Inflation has now been brought under control and there is great progress in scientific and technological research, despite the small budgets available.

Immigration and emigration

Immigration has always been a key to Israel's success. The numbers of immigrants to and emigrants from Israel has fallen in recent years.

Between 1948 and 1968, 45.5 percent of immigrants were from Europe and America, and 54.5 percent from Asia and Africa. In 1985, 72.5 percent came from Asia and Africa. In the 1990s it is expected that many immigrants will be coming from the Soviet Union. The cultural traditions of the newer Israelis are often very different from those of Israel's founders, producing more change.

The search for peace

The last 40 years in Israel have seen no less than six wars. These conflicts have several times threatened world peace. Israel and its neighbors desperately need peace and security.

At the root of the problem is the need for agreement about a separate state for Palestinian Arabs. Within Israel, opinion about what is to be done is bitterly divided. Some Israelis would like to see talks between Israel and the Palestinian Liberation Organization, now that the PLO has officially said they will renounce terrorism and recognize Israel's right to exist. These Israelis would be prepared to consider a separate Palestinian state. Other Israelis believe Israel must continue to hold the Occupied Territories in order to ensure its survival. In the meantime, the strife continues in the Occupied Territories. Many of the world's most powerful countries are eager to see peace in the Middle East. If the desert can be made to bloom, perhaps the years of war can be made to yield a lasting peace.

Index

© Heinemann Children's Reference 1990

This edition originally published 1990 by
Heinemann Children's Reference, a division
of Heinemann Educational Books, Ltd.